Unsolved

Disappearances

(Volume 1)

Gerald Burns

D0999284

OTHER SERIES BY THE AUTHOR

Unexplained, Unsolved, Unsealed Mysteries of the World Book 1 – 6

Ghosts, Poltergeists and Haunted Locations

Unsolved Mysteries + Cup of Coffee = Chill: Notebook for Mystery Lovers (120 Pages)

Table of Contents

Introduction

The M-Cave Adventure

An avid hiker sets out on a mission to find a strange cave. An ominous YouTube comment warns him not to go ahead with his mission, explaining that he would not survive the experience. The hiker goes on his expedition anyway and vanishes into thin air. What happened to him, and why was the mysterious comment deleted after his disappearance?

The Boy with the Hatchet

Just three weeks before Christmas, a grandfather, his son-in-law, and grandson go in search of the perfect pine tree for some Christmas decoration. During this trip, the 8-year-old boy disappeared mysteriously after leaving his grandfather to be with his father just a short distance away. What happened to him that snowy December afternoon?

Finding the City of Z

A renowned explorer hacks his way through one of the densest forests in the world. He believes there is a lost city waiting to be found somewhere in the uncharted area. When no one hears from him for two years, they raise an alarm about his disappearance. Did he go into the forest to start a new religion, or did people of a local tribe abduct him?

I need your flashlight.

A lovely trio on a road trip is attacked by a man they'd befriended at their last stop. Imagine the shock that cruised through their bodies when they found out he was a cold murderer willing to do anything to get their cash, even taking their little girl away permanently.

Taken by the Devil himself

One man mysteriously disappears from his corridor without a trace. How did someone paralyze from the waist down to the lower extremities vanish from his seat, leaving nothing but a blanket? Did he leave to start a new life far away, or did Satan and his cohorts abduct him?

The M-Cave Adventure

An avid hiker sets out on a mission to find a strange cave. An ominous YouTube comment warns him not to go ahead with his mission, explaining that he would not survive the experience. The hiker goes on his expedition anyway and vanishes into thin air. What happened to him, and why was the mysterious comment deleted after his disappearance?

*

The Mojave Desert, located in California, USA, is the hottest and driest among the four major American deserts. It occupies 48,000 sq. miles and contains different landscapes ranging from deep valleys to mountainous landscapes that harbor a variety of wildlife. The desert is home to some tourist locations, such as the place referred to as the Death Valley. Hikers and adventurers are in love with its endless network of underground caves and its assortment of abandoned encampments that can be seen along the way as you explore deeper. It is safe to say that the exploration of this dry place is not for the weak-hearted or the inexperienced.

There are many stories about hikers who ventured into the Mojave Desert to explore it, but they never made it back alive. The same thing happened to 47-year-old Kenny Veach, who told his family he was going on a short adventure in the desert but never returned. His case stands out from the rest due to the awkward events that preceded his journey. This includes a series of YouTube comments detailing his experience in the desert and a warning from an unknown user about the trip. Here is the story of Kenny Veach, the hiker who disappeared in the Mojave Desert.

The Part-time YouTuber

Kenny Veach's story begins on YouTube, where his channel is 'snakebitmgee', a name that alludes to his love of rattlesnakes and his obsession with playing with them. However, he wasn't known for his uploads more than his active followership and commentating on popular hiking vlogs hosted on the platform. He was an avid hiker and explorer, and he spent most of his time around the Mojave and Great Basin deserts in Nevada. Kenny often went on these trips alone with supplies that could last him for hours or overnight. He never felt the need to take a compass or a GPS tracker on these journeys believing that he knew enough about the environment to find his way around. He would also embark on these trips with his then-girlfriend, who was not as daring as him. Despite some of her warnings, Kenny continued to make shabby preparations for his desert trips.

His comments on YouTube reflect his personality and give a glimpse into his weird adventures. One of his comments on an Area 51 video told of his solo hikes across mountains where he would find and play with dangerous rattlesnakes for fun. Another comment narrated how he discovered skulls of various shapes and sizes and old animal traps that had caught nothing for their owners. One time he had gotten stranded in the desert until a helicopter came to rescue him. He had a pretty solid safety record, so, to him, there was no outdoor challenge he couldn't wither. That was until he discovered the M-cave.

The Discovery of the M-Cave

In June 2014, Kenny Veach watched a video uploaded by a user known as 'Son of an area 51 technician'. Kenny left a well-detailed note about his experience around Nellis Air Force Base, Nevada, in the comment section. His YouTube comment on that video narrated how he'd found a hidden cave with an opening shaped like a capital letter. M. Kenny said that he would always enter and explore every new cave he found during his adventure, and this one was no exception. But something strange happened just as he got closer to the cave's entrance. His whole body began to vibrate, and it only got worse as he approached closer. He described it as one of the craziest things that had ever happened to him outdoors.

That comment would spark a four-month interaction from other visitors to the videos who replied to Kenny and challenged him to return to that cave and document his experience. Many of them asked him to take a camera with him and post the video on his channel.

The M-cave that Kenny talked about is located somewhere in the Sheep Mountains, a little north of Las Vegas. The area is quite dangerous and is full of old mine shafts disposed of by the military.

There have been many reports about the area being used by drug cartels to cook their products and host business meetings. Others say that killers travel up to that point to dump their victims.

The second trip, a mysterious comment, and the disappearance

Despite all of these, Kenny still traveled to the area to prove to his skeptics that he was telling this truth. He drove up to the desert with his Rutger 9mm gun and made a complete recording of his journey to and fro the place. This happened on October 18th, 2014, and that mini-documentary is still up for viewing on YouTube with the title, 'M Cave Hike.'

Kenny parked his truck close to the Joe May Canyon and began his search for the M-cave. Hours passed, and it became apparent that he would be unsuccessful at finding this cave. Once he posted the video on YouTube, he received even more negative comments from people who claimed he was lying for clout, with some saying he was looking for a way to draw attention to his channel and grow his following. One of the comments even asked him to kill himself.

Kenny posted another video on YouTube where he stated his intentions to return to the area and search for the mysterious cave again. He asked anyone interested to come out and join him on the adventure, but nobody showed any interest. This time, one comment stood out from the rest, posted by one Lemmy Kilmister. It said, "No! Do not go back there. If you find that cave entrance, don't go in. If you do, you won't get out." Kenny replied to the comment by asking, "What makes you say that?" But his question never received any response from Lemmy.

On November 10th, 2014, Kenny kissed his girlfriend goodbye and told family members he was going on another hiking expedition as usual. They bid him farewell, and that was the last time anyone saw Kenny. When he did not return home by the 14th of November, his girlfriend reported him missing, and the search ensued.

Finding Kenny

Almost a week later, Kenny remained missing, and authorities decided to intensify their search. Volunteers came out in their numbers and formed a larger team to cover a vast area than before. During this operation, members of the Red Rock Search and Rescue team found his cellphone lying close to a mineshaft entrance. This led many to believe that Kenny had ventured into the opening where he fell to his death. Cameras were sent down to investigate the situation of things, but images retrieved did not suggest any form of disturbance from a fall. All was calm and untouched in there, plus there was no sign of a corpse lying around. Apart from his phone, nothing else was found among Kenny's belongings.

By this time, the news of Kenny's disappearance had not reached his online community on YouTube. His followers on the platform still awaited his return with a video to prove that the M-cave was real. They received news of his disappearance in December 2014 when Kenny's girlfriend left a comment on his page, informing them about his disappearance and the ongoing search.

The disappearance instantly became an online sensation as other vloggers began to unearth relevant comments on their page to shed more light on the situation. Some remembered the sinister comment from Lemmy Kilmister, but he had already deleted it.

Suspicions grew, and people wondered what could have happened to the experienced hiker out there in the dangerous terrains of Mojave Desert.

Theories about Kenny's disappearance

Kenny's disappearance has been subject to many speculations and theories. The most popular amongst these is the case of misadventure. Some believed that he may have succumbed to and died of natural causes. As stated earlier, Kenny never took enough precautions when going on any of his hiking trips, plus he believed that such navigational instruments like compasses were for the inexperienced. These unnecessary risks may have landed him in trouble during this outing. He may have lost his way and become disoriented before dying of exhaustion. In some of his videos, Kenny clearly explained that he would sometimes carry as little as some chocolate bars when going to the desert. In his words, "I like to rough it like that." Some say he was bitten by a rattlesnake or attacked by a mountain lion but recall that he had his gun with him on this occasion. And even if any of these attacks killed him, then why didn't the search team find traces of his body. There was no blood on his phone or any sign of struggle between the two entities. Others speculate that Kenny may have seen something he wasn't to see, in this case, a drug deal or some classified military activity, and he was gunned down instantly to keep him shut. Yet, there is no evidence to be sure of this. If such had happened, his attackers would have taken his phone along with his body.

Next up is the theory of escape to start up a new life somewhere else. Later investigations revealed that Kenny had left his former job to start a business that did not flourish as much as he thought it would. It is possible that he owed people money and was trying to run away from it, but there is no evidence to back this claim. Kenny once said he had plans to sell off his home in one of his videos because he was running out of capital for his business. That suggests that he was having some financial trouble at the time. The theory doesn't hold much when you realize the love and care Kenny enjoyed around him. He had a loving family and a girlfriend who he was planning to marry. It is inconceivable that he would allow these people to go through the pain of having him listed as a missing person. Also, the process of disappearing and changing one's identity requires many financial resources that Kenny did not have. His bank account did not show that he had withdrawn a large sum before leaving for his adventure.

Then there is the suicide issue. Recall that Kenny experienced a lot of negative backlash on YouTube after failing to find the M-cave on his second trip. It is possible that his inability to find the cave the third time drove him to near insanity that made him contemplate life as a whole. Some believe he dropped his phone somewhere far and found another mineshaft where he threw himself in and died, making it almost impossible to locate the particular mineshaft and find his body.

The suicide theory is corroborated by a comment by Kenny's girlfriend (Sheryon Pilgrim) left under one of his videos titled 'M Cave Hike.' As of September 2021, the comment already has over 23,000 likes on YouTube. Sheryon said that she didn't believe Kenny had an accident. She thinks that her boyfriend took his life. She revealed his struggle with depression for a year and talked about him quitting his job and selling some of his inventions. Kenny's father had taken his life when his son was only in his 20s, so Sheryon feared he would follow the same path. He'd always told her about his intention, saying that he would never do it in the house but in the wilderness where no one would find his body.

While searching his apartment for clues after his disappearance, investigators came across his internet search history that contained questions regarding suicide methods. Sheryon also claimed that Kenny never took his video camera on the third trip, so there is no proof that he wanted to video anything. Many doubted her relationship with Kenny until Sheryon uploaded a two minutes video titled 'Memories with Kenny Snakebitmgee' on her YouTube channel. The video is enough proof that she'd spent time with the missing hiker.

We cannot conclude the study of these theories without asking about the comment from Lemmy Killmister. What did it mean, and why was the comment deleted after Kenny's disappearance? This aspect of the chilling story only makes this mystery a little stranger than others.

Many other people have tried to find this cave and failed. Go on YouTube, and you will come across hundreds of hikers and explorers who have taken it upon themselves to find the M-cave. One other of them had a serious injury during his trip and had to stop his expeditions. The question remains: does this cave even exist? If it does, then why hasn't anyone found it almost seven years after Kenny's disappearance? Did someone wait for him during his third search and kill or abduct him to shut him up before concealing the cave's entrance from the public's eye? The questions are all mind boggling, and we may never be able to answer them.

What we know for sure is that Nevada and its vast desert is home to some of the most classified locations in America. Perhaps the cave was a secret entrance to one of these locations until Kenny discovered it and let the word out. There are many conspiracy theories about some of these installations, including stories about strange experimentations on abducted human subjects. Perhaps the authorities in charge of that location used some form of ultra-low frequency sound waves to create these vibrations at the entrance and prevent trespassers from venturing any further into the encampment.

Then there is the issue of alien abduction. Nevada is home to some of the most famous UFO interactions, including the one experienced by Charles James Hall, an ex-US airman who documented his encounter with an alien race known as the Tall Whites in his book *Millennial Hospitality*. Charles revealed that this alien race had entered an agreement with the US government to run a secret facility somewhere in the Mojave Desert. Could it be that the M-cave was an entrance to this facility, and Kenny stumbled on something he was never supposed to see? That is a question that we might never get an answer to.

The Boy with the Hatchet

Just three weeks before Christmas, a grandfather, his son-in-law, and grandson go in search of the perfect pine tree for some Christmas decoration. During this trip, the 8-year-old boy disappeared mysteriously after leaving his grandfather to be with his father just a short distance away. What happened to him that snowy December afternoon?

*

Derrick Engebretson became conversant with the ideal peace associated with woodland areas from as little as two years old. His family lived in such an environment, so many of his senior relatives enjoyed taking long walks in the area. As a child, his parents would take him on short trips in the woodlands, teaching him all they knew about surviving in the outdoors. The more Derrick explored with them, the greater his love for the forests became.

Born in 1990 as the third child to parents Robert and Laurie Engebretson, the boy grew so accustomed to the woodland area that he got the nickname 'Bear Boy' bestowed on him by family and friends. It is safe to say he knew his way around the place. He would often join his father, Robert Engebretson, on short adventures in the mountainous terrain to hunt small animals or cut down pine trees for Christmas decorations. Derrick also had a close relationship with his maternal grandfather, who took him on many woodland trips before his sudden disappearance.

Pine Search

Derrick's main story starts in 1998, in the heart of winter that year. The search for Christmas trees had become a yearly tradition for the family, but on this occasion, Derrick and his father were out to find the perfect pine for one of their disabled neighbors since his mother opted for an artificial tree that year.

8-year-old Derrick, his father, and grandfather left their home on December 5th 1998, around 2 pm that afternoon, and started their journey to the Winema National Forest, Oregon, where they believed they would find the perfect pine. On their way there, Robert informed the trio that they would have to find and cut down the selected tree as fast as possible so they could be at their home before dark.

On arriving in the forest, Robert helped his son get into a blue snow coat, and the three of them set out towards the steep area of mountainside Pelican Butte.

Being stronger and more experienced than the other two, Derrick's father decided to leave them behind and move ahead to look around. By now, it was snowing again, something Derrick loved to experience during his outings with his parents. He had a hatchet with him which he used to chop at the trunk of some small trees on their way. Somewhere along the path, Derrick informed his grandfather that he wanted to move faster and catch up with his father. Bob reckoned that his son-in-law was only a short distance away, so he allowed his grandson to speed up and meet his father ahead. Excited by the permission, the little boy ran off until he disappeared from his grandfather's gaze, swallowed up by the greenery up ahead. That was the last time anyone saw him.

Bob finally caught up with Robert about 30 minutes later. Robert asked about the whereabouts of his son, but the father-in-law was shocked to receive the question. He told Robert that Derrick had run ahead of him, so he expected the boy to be somewhere around playing with a hatchet. Robert denied seeing his son, and it was they realized that the little boy was nowhere to be found.

Finding Derrick

By now, the falling snow had become denser, and darkness was covering the area. Robert and Bob searched around the place and followed the trail back to the car, looking for Derrick. They screamed his name and called out to him, but they received no response. All they met was silence, pure silence and darkness covering the embankment. The two of them looked for the boy for over an hour before they realized the gravity of the situation. It was almost pitch black by now.

Confused with the situation, Robert decided to run down to the road, where he flagged down a good Samaritan and asked them to inform the police about the disappearance. The police were contacted, but they arrived at the scene relatively late, almost three hours later. Worst of all, they didn't come with a search team since the local search crew had its end of the year banquet, and they didn't want to end the occasion abruptly. The

Oregon State Police only put together a small search team to scour the area and see what they could find until the main team joined them after their party. They searched for the boy all through that night until the following day with sniffer dogs and snowmobiles while helicopters scanned from above using thermal imaging and the likes. Derrick remained missing.

The search was made even more difficult since it was being conducted in darkness. By the following day, significant clues such as footprints in the snow were heavily blanketed due to the weather condition at the time. It made it almost impossible to trace the place Derek had been as he wandered off the path that led to his father.

A glimpse of hope fell on the search party when they discovered a small shelter built out of fir boughs near the place Derrick parted with his grandfather. The police were led to believe that perhaps Derrick had made the shelter to protect himself from the elements after he lost his way. Sniffer dogs were brought to shelter for confirmation's sake, but none of the dogs could find any trace of the little boy.

Another hope came in the form of a snow angel discovered close to an embankment, and it looked like one formed by a small person. Close to the snow angel was evidence of Derrick's footprints tracing a path down the hill towards the road that passed at the bottom. The search team followed these prints until they reached the road where they disappeared abruptly, without any sign that its owner had turned the other way. This led some people to insinuate that the boy had been abducted close to the road, but the police said that there wasn't enough evidence to be certain of that. Although, a snowplow had worked through the area in the passing days and cleared up any other footprints.

Further traces of the boy's whereabouts were discovered when members of the search saw chopped tree barks lying around in the snow. Authorities had enough reasons to believe that the missing boy chopped them since he had a hatchet at the time of his disappearance. Some footprints believed to be his were also discovered at the bank of a frozen lake with a hole. Divers were summoned and asked to seek his body, but their search presented nothing promising.

It got to a point where Mrs. Lori Engebretson left home with her family and camped around where her son had gone missing. They all stayed in a donated camper van as they scavenged the forest day and night, searching for their child. At night they lit a fire near the van to help guide Derrick to them. Lori's mental stress became so much that she claimed she could see Derrick coming towards the van one night, waving and smiling at his family. Family members went out to check, but it turned out she was hallucinating.

Search volunteers later found a candy wrapper somewhere around his trail and a bookmark bearing the name of Derrick's school. Sadly, officials were unable to connect these objects to the missing boy. Bloodstains on snow were also found around the location, but they could not determine if it belonged to an animal or a human being.

After a grueling eight days, search parties decided to call off the search for the safety of the volunteers. They had experienced multiple blizzards during those days, and some of them harbored reasonable fear for their health. Authorities now believed Derrick was dead because no child his age could have survived terrible conditions unsupervised by an older person.

Despite the call-off, his family continued to search the area alone until they decided to return home on December 18th because of the unbearable weather condition. Authorities concluded that Derrick had died due to the harsh weather or a wild beast had attacked him, but Robert and Lori Engebretson remained convinced that their son had been abducted, and they were determined to find traces to prove this.

Speculations and accusations

One person came forward with little information from the day of the disappearance. The witness, in this case, claimed that they had seen an unidentified man struggling with a little boy close to the area where Derrick went missing. The witness claimed they didn't raise any alarm since it looked like a normal father and son situation. Other investigations suggested that the same man owned a black Honda car and people claimed he seemed lost and asked them for directions on how to get away from the forest. This man was never identified, and it remains unclear what transpired that cold afternoon.

Apart from the physical and mental torture that Lori and her husband experienced due to their son's disappearance, there was also the financial problem that came with it. The couple put in so much of their money to find their son, ranging from such commitments as paying divers to get into cold lakes and find his body to consulting psychic mediums in the hope of locating their boy. Soon enough, they ran out of financial resources and were forced to pause the search until they regained stability. Robert Engebretson suffered severe pneumonia during those years due to the hours spent in the snow, digging desperately to find closure for himself and the family.

The police had no new leads to explore within a year, and the case started going cold. But not for the Engebretson family who returned to the area for months to search in their spare time.

It is safe to say that some locals were harsh towards the family as they began peddling rumors that Derrick's relatives had a hand in his disappearance. These were unfounded, but people being who they are, continued to push them even though they had no evidence to back them up. Both Robert and Bob Engebretson took lie-detector tests that cleared them from any of these suspicions.

An Offensive Graffiti

Something later popped up on September 24th, 1999, in the form of graffiti found in a public toilet around Portland. The graffiti revealed some details about Derrick's disappearance, but its content was never released to the public. Investigators took it as a new lead to explore but soon discovered it was only a hoax that would lead nowhere meaningful. It was only a testament to the cruelness of people who wanted to play a practical joke on the grieving family.

Frank Milligan

In 2004, authorities handling the case revealed that they had a suspect they were looking into. His name was Frank Milligan, and this suspect had attacked and sexually molested an 11-year-old boy in Dallas, Oregon, before slashing his throat. Thankfully, his victim survived the assault. But Frank did not stop there. He also attacked another boy later that year, after which he was sentenced to 35 years in prison.

A fellow inmate of Milligan told police that Milligan once confessed to him about killing Derrick Engebretson. It is believed that Milligan picked him along the road where the last footprints were seen before murdering the little child.

During interrogation, Milligan admitted to murdering the boy but said he would plead guilty if he was spared from the death penalty. When asked to lead investigators to the burial site, Milligan failed to locate where he buried the body. A search team arrived and swept through the surrounding area looking for Derrick's corpse. They were only able to recover a couple of bones that belonged to dead animals.

After the episode, Milligan recanted his confession and kept mute about the issue, not saying another word to the police about his involvement. Though he was never charged for killing Derrick, Milligan remains a prime suspect in the case to date. He once owned a black Honda car that looked similar to the one the witness saw around the woodland where Derrick went missing.

Two decades have gone by without any trace of Derrick Engebretson, but his mother still believes that her son is alive and well out there and he will return to her one day. All of the Christmas celebrations without Derrick have been painful to bear, but his mother has remained the rock of the household as the years go by. Derrick's grandfather, Bob, who was the last person to see him alive, sadly passed away in 2012, without knowing what happened that fateful day.

As for description, Derrick Engebretson is a Caucasian boy with hazel-colored eyes. He stood at about 4ft before his disappearance. There were several scars on his face, all caused by dog bites. He was last seen holding a hatchet that has not been seen since 1998.

Finding the City of Z

A renowned explorer hacks his way through one of the densest forests in the world. He believes there is a lost city waiting to be found somewhere in the uncharted area. When no one hears from him for two years, they raise an alarm about his disappearance. Did he go into the forest to start a new religion, or did people of a local tribe abduct him?

*

May 2025 will mark 100 years since Percy Fawcett was swallowed up in one of the largest forests in South America. For most of his life, Percy enjoyed the thrill of being referred to as a successful explorer. A few years before his disappearance, he began nurturing an obsession with an ancient civilization he claimed once existed somewhere in the Amazon. Percy made it his lifelong goal to find this city which he fondly referred to as 'The Lost

City of Z.' He didn't have a clue that his search for the lost city would eventually lead to his disappearance and an enduring mystery that would haunt family members and the British government for years to come.

Who was Percy Fawcett before the infamous expedition?

Lieutenant Colonel Percival Fawcett was born on the 18th of August, 1867 in Devon, England. His father had an interesting history, popular among the natives as a drunk gambler who had nearly succeeded in squandering most of his inherited net worth. This characteristic caused Percy to view his father with mild disdain.

Percy nurtured an ambition from a little age while growing up in the era of great explorers and adventurers. He had his childhood education at Newton Abbot Proprietary school before being commissioned as a member of the Royal Geographical Society. Fawcett was later posted to the British Colony of Ceylon as an officer of the Royal Artillery. Around this time, he met and fell in love with a lady (Nina Agnes Paterson), who he married and bore two sons – Jack and Brian Fawcett. Throughout his stay in the colony, Percy remained an explorer, hunting and seeking lost or buried treasures anywhere on the land.

Percy occasionally returned home due to injuries, and at some point, it seemed pointless to send him back to Ceylon. At 39, he was given a fully-funded offer by the Royal Geographical Society to explore and map out the jungle border of Brazil and Bolivia, which was referred to as 'blank spaces' at the time. Fawcett knew and acknowledged the fact that his new assignment was one of the most dangerous ever undertaken by an explorer in British history, but the excitement of it caused him to accept the challenge.

His former expeditions had taken him around the world as he created maps to some of the most isolated jungles in vast continents. In 1906, Fawcett set out on a journey to the South American continent. After his return, he claimed to have seen a 62-foot anaconda he shot but didn't kill. The story sounded outrageous, and fellow explorers and adventurers mocked him and called him a conman looking for easy accolades. Percy did not allow their words to get to him as he continued to dish out stories about his encounters. He spoke about the Bolivian Mitla, which he described as a medium-sized cat-looking dog that lived in the Brazilian rainforest, and the giant Apazauca spider. Fawcett also told historians that he'd seen doubled-nosed dogs around the forest in 1913. Researchers have come to believe that he was probably referring to the double-nosed Andean tiger hounds.

His peculiar exploits as an explorer earned him numerous accolades among his colleagues while making it to headlines worldwide. It was during this time that Fawcett received a medal from the Royal Geographical Society. He also became friends with influential figures such as authors H. Rider Haggard and Sir Arthur Conan Doyle, both inspired by his tales to write successful novels in the early 1900s, including the 1912 novel by Doyle titled *The Lost World*.

The Lost City of Z

After a series of successful trips to and fro the forests of South America, Fawcett started to tell people about his belief in the existence of an ancient city buried in ruins somewhere around the Amazon. He also believed that the former inhabitants of this place had experienced so much wealth and rich culture to rival the Romans and the Greeks. When questioned about the possibility of that, Fawcett cited the survival of native Indians in the area as proof that any other group could survive there as well.

His conviction was further strengthened when he came across a document known as *Manuscript 512* with a dubious and outrageous history. The document gave information about discovering some ruins around 1753, although it had no verifiable author information. It contained detailed sketches of a statue and a temple with hieroglyphics. Sadly, there was not a single piece of information regarding the location of these ruins, which made it all the more intriguing to Fawcett and his team.

As he made more journeys to the Amazon, Fawcett became increasingly obsessed with finding this city in ruins, referring to it as his El Dorado and dubbing it The Lost City of Z.

The first two searches for this city ended abruptly due to terrible weather conditions, illnesses and stress. With each failed trip, Fawcett found it increasingly harder to convince his sponsors that he wasn't wasting their resources on some fantastical adventure. It is important to note that Fawcett encountered many natives in the area during his expedition and his teammates were hellbent on treating them as savages, but Fawcett would not have it. He disagreed with the approach and ensured that the locals were respected on their land. He would arrive in the jungle bearing gifts for the elders of the various tribes. Many times, these kind gestures would help him gain passage through some hostile territories.

By the time Fawcett was ready to embark on his third trip in search of the Lost City, he had discovered he had run out of funds for the journey. This led to three years of campaigning from door to door in search of funding. Luckily enough, he found someone ready to listen to his outlandish idea and provide resources for the journey.

Journey to the Lost City

Fawcett set off on his journey to the Lost City sometime in 1925 after receiving funding from an organization in London who referred to themselves Glove. He embarked on that trip with his son, Jack, and his close friend, Raleigh Rimell. This would turn out to be his last foray into the foreign world.

In Brazil, he hired the help of two laborers among the locals and paid for two horses, eight mules, and some dogs to help with the luggage. But somewhere along the way, Fawcett reduced his party to include just him, his son, and his friend, Rimell. He has been described as a fit and healthy man even at 57, and he'd always stayed away from alcohol and meat, believing them to be detrimental to his health. For this trip, he needed to have only healthy people accompany him into the thickest parts of the jungle since most of his other explorations had been cut short due to the failing health of some people in his party. He didn't want that to be a hindrance again. Before heading further, Fawcett left a warning that no one should try to come and find him if he did not return. He was so confident in his ability to discover the lost city that he reckoned no one else would be able to find it if someone as zealous as him failed.

Fawcett would occasionally send letters home to his wife detailing his experience. The last among the letters was sent on May 29th 1925. The letter sounded optimistic and revealed information about his current location, which he called the Dead Horse Camp. He seemed to vanish into thin air after sending that letter. Nearly two years later, there was still no news from the Colonel. Once hailed as one of the most daring explorers of his time, Fawcett now became an object of intense speculation regarding his whereabouts.

Searching for Fawcett

The Royal Geographical Society launched a search for Colonel Fawcett in late 1927. The head of the team, George Miller Dyott, returned from the investigation with no good news. He believed that the expedition team had met their death in the jungle, and their bodies had been undiscovered. No one can tell how well he searched for these men out there in the Amazon. Nina Fawcett believed that her husband and his team were alive, saying that no one had provided enough proof of their deaths.

Since Fawcett's disappearance, many other explorers have ventured into South America to find any trace to his whereabouts. It is estimated that about 80 of these people have lost their lives in the heart of the forest while searching for the Colonel, even though he specifically stated that he wanted no one to come after him in case he went missing. All of these people simply vanished in the

Amazon, the same way the man they were looking for had vanished. One of the most recent among these defiant rescue teams was led by popular Brazilian businessman James Lynch in 1996. Lynch and his team encountered a tribe of Amazonian Indians who captured them after a brief battle. They were only released after letting go of some of their most prized possessions and allowed to return home with nothing. The brother of Ian Fleming, author of the James Bond books, is also among those explorers who searched for Fawcett. He is lucky to be counted among the few that returned home alive.

Most Popular Theories about Fawcett's Disappearance

As is expected, many theories have been put forward to explain what could have happened to the group of British explorers. Many have asked if they got lost and died from starvation. Some say that they were attacked by anacondas or wild beasts that devoured them. Others believe that they got trapped and died in an isolated location in the forest.

One theory that started gaining ground in 2004 was put forward by theater director Misha Williams. Williams had approached Brain Fawcett, the Colonel's second son, seeking permission to go through his father's papers. Brian allowed him access to these documents, including letters, diaries, and other writing. From his research and study, Misha concluded that Fawcett and his party had founded a spiritual commune in the jungle with the locals. Misha claimed that the contents of Fawcett's writing made him believe that this commune was based on theosophical principles and the worship of his son, Jack. This claim sounds less outrageous when we consider that Edward Fawcett, the Colonel's elder brother, was also a practitioner of theosophy which is regarded as an occultic movement that believes in reincarnation and the existence of Karma.

Of course, the most sensible among these claims was the team being murdered by hostile Indians in the area. The Kalapalo tribe was accused of this atrocity since they occupied most of the place Fawcett had headed towards with his team. In 1950, an activist for the rights of indigenous people of Brazil, Orlando Villa-Boas, reported that the tribe had indeed killed the explorer. His story went that members of the tribe had found Fawcett and his men sick and dying. They had then decided to kill them to ease their pain. He said that the other men were thrown into a nearby river, but Fawcett was given a befitting burial, seeing that he was a distinguished personality.

When asked for evidence to support his claims, the activist said the tribe had given him Fawcett's bones. A test was conducted to verify his claims, but Brian Fawcett rejected the results and branded them false. Villa-Boas then accused the family of prolonging the story of the disappearance since they loved the publicity associated with it. A few years later, another set of tests were carried out on the bones, and this time it was concluded that they didn't belong to the missing colonel. In 1980, an elder of the tribe discredited the story and called Villa-Boas a liar looking to profit off the story. This was all recorded during an interview with BBC. The elder told the world that his tribe had nothing to do with Fawcett's disappearance.

More than 50 years later, elders of the tribe continue to hold on to their story that they had nothing to do with Fawcett's death. David Grann, writer of the bestselling book *The Lost City of Z* traveled to the area in 2009 to question the elders himself. They told him the same thing, that none of their ancestors had even come across the three explorers.

There are claims that Fawcett was warned not to venture towards a certain territory since that place was home to some hostile Indians. Rumor has it that he disregarded his advice and went towards that path anyway. Some locals say that they used to see a fire afar off every night that showed where Fawcett and his men had reached. For five nights, the lights appeared until it didn't appear one day, and no one ever saw it again.

In recent years, evidence has come out that proves Fawcett may have had a point with his claims of a lost city in the Amazon. Archeologists now have reasons to believe that many sophisticated settlements existed in the ancient Amazon, some of which were wiped off by European invasion. Research and excavation have revealed city defensive systems and complex road networks around the area. Some of these were discovered around the same area Fawcett said he would be going to search.

I need your flashlight.

A lovely trio on a road trip is attacked by a man they'd befriended at their last stop. Imagine the shock that cruised through their bodies when they found out he was a cold murderer willing to do anything to get their cash, even taking their little girl away permanently.

*

Born on May 24th 1946, 15-year-old Denise Sullivan resided with her mother, Miss. Jeannette D. Sullivan and her little sister, in Rockville, Connecticut. Miss. Jeannette had just gone through a messy divorce, and she was working as a seamstress to support herself and her two daughters.

Sometime in 1961, Miss. Jeannette, who was 41 at the time, met and fell in love with 51-year-old Charles E. Boothroyd. Their relationship remained stable throughout the year, and they soon started making plans to officialize their union. It was around this time that Charles came to his fiancée with a mouth-watering offer. He wanted the soon-to-be family to embark on a vacation trip to Utah in the summer of that year. Jeannette and Denise (sometimes called Denny) agreed to his proposition and decided to join him for the holiday trip. They dropped off the youngest daughter with Jeannette's parents, and the other three embarked on a journey that none of them would return from, unfortunately.

The Man on the Highway

The three travelers drove down to Utah in Charles' Volkswagen. On the 4th of July 1961, the trio met a heavyset man with a thick beard around Dead Horse Points in Utah. Believing that he knew enough about the area, they spent about two hours in conversation with this man, asking him questions about the place and taking some pictures of the environment.

As it got darker, the man told them he would be on his way since he had other businesses to settle in the next town. He quickly got into his Sedan and drove off without telling any of them his name. Since they were planning to spend the night in a motel in Moab, Charles and Jeannette decided it would be best to leave and began their journey there as quickly as possible. They got into Charles' car and left the place, too.

Somewhere along the line, almost halfway through their journey, they came across this same man with thick beards packed by the side of the road. He was lying under his car, and it seemed he was having some issues with the engine or something.

Charles and Jeanette decided to stop and offer as much help as they could to their new friend. They pulled over close to the sedan and asked the man what the problem was and if they could offer some assistance. The man said it was only a minor issue but asked if they could help him with their flashlight. Jeannette walked back to the car and retrieved the flashlight from her bag, and then returned to hand it over to the man.

At this point, the couple knew that they had made a mistake by stopping over to offer some help. Once the man had the flashlight in his hand, he pulled out a .22 caliber rifle and began threatening the family and asking them to produce all the money they had on them. Charles obeyed instantly by finding his wallet and throwing it to the man. Jeannette, on the other hand, dug her hands into her purse and handed him $250. Then the couple turned and tried to walk away from the scene, but it seemed like the man had more sinister plans. He shot Jeannette at the back of her head, killing her instantly, and Charles received two bullets, but he managed to survive his injury.

In a panic fit, the man proceeded to pull Jeannette's body off the road into a nearby ravine. He left Charles lying there on the floor, bleeding profusely.

The young girl, Denny, had seen everything that transpired from where she was sitting in the car. Fearing for her life and safety, she threw herself into the driver's seat in a bid to drive off and save herself from this demented killer. The man soon noticed the car's movements and tried to reach the driver's seat and stop her from taking off, but it was too late. Denny succeeded in putting the car into gear and driving off. He quickly got into his car and gave chase. Somewhere along the line, the man caught up with the young girl and eventually managed to run her off the road. He got out of his car and dragged her out of the Volkswagen into his Sedan.

The Search for Denny

There was a construction site close to the location of the assault, and one of the oil workers on the site heard the gunshots from over two miles away. He was intrigued by the disturbing sound and decided to investigate the issue. According to him, he'd passed a car at high speed moving in the opposite direction but thought nothing of it. He saw Charles' damaged Volkswagen packed along the road where Denny had been abducted on his way there. Further down, he found Charles bleeding profusely on the road.

Charles narrated the ordeal he had just faced, and the oil worker decided to seek help. Soon enough, an ambulance arrived and took Charles away, and authorities began the unending search for Denny Sullivan. They searched day and night, ransacking the area to find a body, at least. Their investigation resulted only in frustration as none of them could find the girl or any trace of her whereabouts.

Benny Aragon

A few days later, police believed that they had a main suspect. He was a 35-year-old Marine veteran named Abel Benny Aragon. Benny was unemployed at the time, and he lived in Price, Utah, close to the location of the attack. His sedan car fitted that of Charles' assailant and the paint stain on the side of his car matched those from the scratches on Charles' Volkswagen. Further investigations also revealed two footprints that matched Aragon's footwear and the other matching Denny's shoes.

Although he had no previous convictions and had been awarded a Navy Cross for heroism during World War II, the police knew that they had enough evidence in their hands to take him down and serve justice.

On the 6th of July, just two days after the assault, a policeman stopped Aragon in his car and asked him to come out for questioning. Aragon pulled out a pistol from somewhere in his car before yelling 'PROVE IT!' and shooting himself in the head. He passed away about two hours later.

During an extensive investigation, police collected several statements from different sources. Many of them stated that they'd seen Benny roaming the area around 3 am the morning after Charles and Jeannette's attack. He was later sighted around the Polar Mesa mining camp, which he'd visited a couple of times before.

The detectives and their team conducted an extensive search of the area and found shocking items. They saw some pieces of clothing and a shovel hidden in a nearby bush. They also found the same rifle used to murder Jeannette. This information was enough for the police to tag Benny Aragon as their man even though he was now dead.

A truck driver came forward with a claim that Benny had given him a letter to mail to a certain location. The letter was successfully intercepted, and the package contained some money and a love note from Benny to his wife and five kids. But it didn't mention any of the crimes committed or anything that could link him to them.

Denny Sullivan remains missing to this day. Authorities have reason to suspect foul play in this case, given its surrounding circumstances. It is most likely she was killed and buried around Polar Mesa, or Benny had struck a deal and sold her off to child traffickers.

At the time of her disappearance, Denny was 15 years old, standing at the height of 5 feet and weighing about 90 pounds. She is of Caucasian descent with brown hair and brown eyes. She would be around 75 years old if found after the year 2020.

Taken by the Devil himself

One man mysteriously disappears from his corridor without a trace. How did someone paralyze from the waist down to the lower extremities vanish from his seat, leaving nothing but a blanket? Did he leave to start a new life far away, or did Satan and his cohorts abduct him?

*

The disappearance of Owen Parfitt is one of the most enduring cases of a person who simply vanished out of sight within seconds. It gets more intriguing when you realize that this man was paralyzed from his waist down and was perpetually needing help to get around the house he shared with his sister. This story has endured since the 18th century and continues to haunt mystery enthusiasts who wonder what happened to Owen. Here is the mysterious account of Owen Parfitt's disappearance.

Owen's Past Life

The first thing you need to know about the main character of this story is that he once lived a wild life before his disappearance. In fact, legend has it that he disappeared twice.

Born during the late 17ᵗʰ century, the young Owen grew up to love sewing and combative sports. He was raised with his sister, Mary Parfitt, in a small English town called Shepton Mallet, where he served under his father as a tailor's apprentice. He was so good at the craft that everyone in the family was sure that the boy would grow up to become a decent tailor. That was until something strange happened that changed the course of his life.

A few years into his twenties, Owen disappeared without telling anyone about his whereabouts, not his family members or friends. Everyone was left in the dark. People who made up the small town came together to find their beloved son, sending messages far and while in search of the young man. Yet, there was nothing tangible to be discovered about him. Rumors swirled around town that Owen had abandoned his family trade to go on an adventure in faraway lands, to experience the world differently. Some said that he'd always complained about the monotonous structure of his everyday life in his father's shop, and he yearned for something better. There was no evidence to back these claims, so the years went by until they became decades, and the town gradually forgot about Owen, remembering him only during conversations. His parents died without ever getting to know what happened to their son.

The Owen Parfitt mystery endured until one more morning in the 1760s when a more mature man strolled into town and announced to everyone who cared to listen that he was the so-called Owen. He returned like nothing had happened, bearing tales of adventures in faraway places.

At first, nobody believed this imposter until his sister was called in to come and confirm if the man was really her brother. On sighting him, she instantly remembered him and confirmed he was her brother.

The Life of a Returnee

After arriving in town, Owen spent most of his days making new friends and telling them about his past conquests. There were stories about his involvement in epic battles and a life of crime as a renowned pirate out at sea. He seemed to have experienced so much of the world within those years when everyone thought he'd gone missing. Among all of this, there was one narrative that stuck out the most. It didn't take long for everyone to realize that Owen Parfitt had become a chronic womanizer. It was evident from his numerous stories about ladies he'd taken to bed and also through his actions in the town he'd now become a part of. He never knew that many people who made up his audience never believed any of his tales.

By this time, he was living with his sister and helping her as a tailor. His years of adventure had taken a toll on him so much that his health suffered the consequences. Owen's posture changed drastically as his body and bones withered. One minute he was a hale and hearty returnee, and the next minute his body was being battered with rheumatism and the effects of past wounds.

Mary's finances suffered since she had to bear the whole weight of taking care of her brother. Many people in the town still believed the man was an imposter looking to make a living off a sad sister, and they advised her to send him off, but she refused. She felt a need to devote her life and money to the care of her younger brother.

Soon enough, they had to move from their home into a smaller cottage at the end of the street with a beautiful garden laid out in front. She believed that the new place would be perfect for an ailing man. She immediately enlisted the help of a young woman called Susannah Snook, who helped with chores around the house and assisted Mary in lifting her brother from the bed to his chair.

Parfitt Vanishes

Owen, Susannah, and Mary lived a quiet life in their new cottage at the end of the street. The two women would lift Owen onto his chair and carry him out to the corridor to receive a little bit of nature's blessing whenever the weather was cool and pleasant. On June 6th 1768, Owen asked to be moved to the corridor once again. It was a cool, windy afternoon, and dark clouds were approaching on the horizon. The two women obeyed the man and moved him to his favorite spot, thinking nothing of the gesture.

Mary stood around the corner chatting with her brother, who sat in the corridor. She never moved more than 20 feet away from him during this time, and he continued to reply to her questions until he simply failed to answer her one more time. Mary repeated her question, yet there was no response. It was at this point she sensed something had gone wrong. She walked out to the corridor to check if her brother was alright, only to get there and find his chair empty without any sign of struggle whatsoever.

Alarmed, Mary walked around the house calling her brother's name, hoping for some miracle or something to explain his strange disappearance. It occurred to her that a neighbor had helped move him into the house, but there was no sign of Owen Parfitt anywhere in their cottage. Even Susannah claimed not to have seen him around the house.

For a minute or two, Mary stood in the corridor and observed the vast scenery before her, wondering how a paralyzed man could have moved from his seat and vanished into thin air.

The Search for Owen Parfitt

When Mary and Susannah discovered that they could not find Owen, they raised the alarm and alerted their neighbors of the new development. None of them claimed to have seen Owen even though it was a summer afternoon and everyone had been out and about during the time. It was probably the busiest time of the year, and it would have been impossible for no one person to notice the disappearance of such an unhealthy man.

Some workers who had been working on a little farm just across the road said they'd seen no one around the house or heard no noise that suggested a struggle. The Parfitt family did not live in an isolated area. In fact, their home was located quite close to a major road that led in and out of town. So, it is shocking that no one noticed anything unusual before his disappearance.

Let's imagine he'd somehow mustered the energy to pull himself from the seat and be on his way to start a new life. It is impossible that he would have moved so far before Mary noticed his absence. Being paralyzed would require him to drag his lower body through the floor as he tried to escape. There is no need to explain the excruciating pain and overall absurdity of that, so the possibility of such an escape is ruled out.

Many of the town people halted their daily activities and joined in the search for the missing man. There had been a heavy thunderstorm the night he disappeared, so they were more in search of a body than to find him alive because it seemed impossible for a paralyzed man to survive for so long on his own. Weeks passed, and it became obvious that Owen was truly gone and may not be found again. His case was gradually tossed aside as the people returned to their lives, hoping that he would return the same way he'd returned after his first disappearance.

Theories and Speculations

There have been many claims put forward by people who have become fascinated by this case. The first and most plausible amongst them is the issue of kidnapping. It is most likely that some people came to that corridor and took Owen away for some reason. But this begs the question of who and why? Well, looking back at Owen's past, it may not be too hard to say. One can conclude that he really hurt many people during his travels and expeditions, and, somehow, they found out where he now lived and came to take him for some punishment. Even at that, there is no way they could have done this successfully without getting him to raise the alarm and alert his sister. Plus, how come no one saw the kidnapping take place? This leads us to the next theory.

This theory suggests that Owen was tired of his new life in the same town and wanted something more, even as an older man. It insinuates that his paralysis had simply been a deceitful game to get his sister to care for him as he hatched his perfect escape plan. This seems like theory until you consider biology. If Owen had succeeded in deceiving his sister for so long, he also would have ended up weakening his unused legs. Remember, he was pretty old at this point, with weak muscles. Let's say he found a way around that; how did no one see him as he tried to escape? The road had been quite busy that day, and some workers were toiling on a farmland just in front of the house. It makes it all stranger.

Others have chosen to believe that Mary had a hand in her brother's disappearance, after which she cooked up a perfect story to cover her tracks.

But why would a woman, who was reportedly close to eighty-five, want to hurt her paralyzed younger brother?

Months after his disappearance, Mary suggested that the Devil and his minions had arrived at her cottage that fateful day and abducted her brother. She believed that all the outrageous activities he had dabbled in had finally caught up with him. Given the strangeness of his disappearance and the height of superstitious beliefs of that era, many people supported her, and the story traveled far and wide that the devil had come to take a man in the small town of Shepton Mallet.

Excitement grew in 1813 when someone who lived close to Parfitt's cottage dug up a human skeleton that had been buried in his garden. It was thought that these remains belonged to Owen until official examination revealed them to be that of a woman. Once again, the world was plunged back into a mystery maze. What happened to Owen Parfitt?